Clotheslines U.S.A.

Clotheslines are signal flags, a story of life written on the wind.

Helen Mather

Clotheslines U.S.A.

Doubleday & Company, Inc., Garden City, New York.

2/16/76

One day it occurred to me that clotheslines of America, like the American buffalo, might one day become extinct. A lot of people talked about clotheslines, but nobody did anything about them. It was up to me.

"It's too late already," said my friends in New York. "The big machines have eaten them up, and besides, everything's plastic."

Nevertheless, I drove out across the country to see for myself. There are plenty of clotheslines left. America is still hung and strung with them. I went from the Atlantic to the Pacific and back again, twelve thousand miles, doing nothing but looking at clotheslines and talking to Americans who have their feet on the ground, their eyes squinting into the sun, and their clothes on the line.

"I just like

air clothes.''

"Pass me some pins from that basket over there," they would say, and proceed to deliver commercials for a product that is absolutely free.

"When I bring my clothes in from the air, I like the way they smell."

"As long as I can make it down those back steps, my clothes will be on the line."

There is a Mrs. Slocum, in the Sacramento Valley of California, who turned from her swinging sheets to me, "There's vitamins in that sun, and when I hang my sheets outdoors, them vitamins get into them sheets, and when I get into them sheets, them vitamins gets into me."

Some areas of America are so backwoodsy that they think a dryer is something you put in paint, but by and large, most women have machines, but use them only in deep winter and during long rainy spells.

This is a large and stubborn section of America, and they will keep the flags flying.
The truth of the matter is that property values, not machines, are the greatest enemy of the clotheslines.

There are housebound women, who see vicarious, outdoor life playing on the line.

"Even if I can't be out myself, I can watch them from the window."

There is great pride, among clothes hangers, to see who can get their wash out first. If you don't live in a close community, you may have to phone your neighbor, on the next farm, to see who is the winner.

My apprehensive friends prepared a speech for me to deliver when I walked into strangers' back yards. It was a very sincere little talk that stated my purpose, gave my identification, and even had a statement from my minister. It took ten minutes.

A Mennonite lady, in Pennsylvania, interrupted me in the middle of it. "'Deed I don't care, long as you are not selling anything."
From then on, I walked into back yards, holding out my empty hands, calling, "I'm not selling anything."

Everything would go very well. I would visit with the lady who was hanging out her wash, but as soon as I remarked casually that I was spending the summer just looking at clotheslines, she would look alarmed.

"Now I've heard everything."

She would measure the distance to the kitchen door, in a quick uneasy glance, in case she had to run.

I would begin telling her how different clotheslines looked in different parts of the country, but I could tell her mind wasn't on it. She was preoccupied, puzzling whether a person should call the dog warden, the fire department, or the police in a case like this.

But when the time came for me to leave, she would walk out to the car with me. When I got in, she would plant her elbows on the window and tell me that if she didn't have a husband and those four boys, she'd come along.

My friend Bea Heddericg wouldn't come along with me. She didn't have to travel. She does her clothesline watching from her own back steps. She claims it's just normal curiosity, but some people say she's got a mite more. She uses binoculars.

Bea gave me my first lessons in researching.

By the time I got to Pittsburgh, I could tell from the clotheslines just about everything there was to know about a family. How many kids, boys, girls, how old they each were, if another was on the way, the family's cash income, what Papa did for a living, Mamma's state of mind, even the family's racial origin.

"If you did something real, like researching," said my friend with I B M , "maybe you could get a grant."

"It looks to me like you've got two boys, Mrs. Watkins. One must be about three, and one about seven."

"That's right," said Mrs. Watkins.

I could tell the ages of the kids from the dungarees, but I always checked out the underpants to tell the girls from the boys. Dungarees all zip down the front, but luckily the drawers are still heterosexual.

"There's a girl about twelve, and another that looks like fourteen."

Mrs. Watkins nodded, so I went on. "Your family is English."

"Scottish," said Mrs. Watkins. "Close enough. How'd you tell?"

"From the handkerchiefs. Mr. Watkins drives a truck."

"Where do you see that?"

"His shirts are worn across the shoulders." At this point Mr. Watkins himself appeared. He came out of the shed and walked up to me.

"Now it's my turn. Can I ask you something?"

"Sure."

"Can you tell a Democrat from a Republican?"

"No."

"I'll tell you. If you are a Republican, there are pajamas on the line. If you are a Democrat, you sleep raw."

"It's woman's stuff," said the sportswriter. "Where do men come in?"

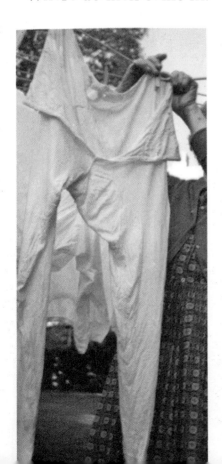

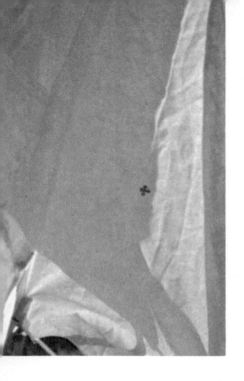

Priest

Fire watcher

Railroad man

Pizza man

Lobsterman

Dirt farmer

"But honey, you're going to miss everything really interesting!" said Grace in the beauty parlor. "Promise me you'll see Disneyland too."

I saw love of craft, religion, politics, census figures, economics, sculpture, drama, poetry, and sex, all on the scattered, unself-conscious clotheslines of America.

Keds over Portland

Uniforms drying over Penobscot Bay

Lace curtains over parking lots

Bloomers over San Francisco

Sugar sacking for somebody's sugar

Dungarees in the sequoias

Potholders in Pennsylvania

There is more than conversation on the party lines
across Oklahoma.

Down the porches

Over the bars

Up the mountains

Around old houses

"Who cares?" He was a paperback editor.
"There's no sex in it."

In the Puerto Rican district of Chicago, I saw two identical skirts drying on the roof of a two-story building. They were cotton skirts, both in the same lurid print. There must be some excuse for two.

"Twins?" I asked a soft-eyed Latin boy holding hands with a soft-eyed Latin girl on the porch, as I pointed to the skirts on the roof.
"No twins," he said.
"Ask your wife if she bought two skirts just alike," I persisted.
"She's not my wife."
"Well then, ask your sister, does she have two skirts just alike?"
"She's not my sister."
"Ask your—friend."
He spoke to the soft-eyed girl, then turned to me. "She says there are three. One is hers, one belongs to my girl friend, but the other one belongs to my wife. She's down the street."
It turned out, believe it or not, that the young man worked at night.

Brassieres over Pittsburgh

I broadcast an appeal from Kirksville, Missouri, for women to tell me where I could see clothes made from feed sacking, and flour sacking and sugar sacking on the lines. The calls poured into the radio station. I went out to find aprons, and dresses, and dish towels, and quilts, everything women had made from sacking before it disappeared from the grocery shelves.

They were all beautiful, but there was one garment that was monumental.
The lady told me she had made it herself, from feed sacking. She went on to say that "It was easier for me than it would be for most girls because I was flat-chested."

It was a brassiere, a size 46.

A sailor, below decks in a freighter off Chicago, did not hang his shorts on the line, he tossed them like quoits. These underpants were quite splendid. One was patterned all over in champagne glasses overflowing. The other was patterned in a design of young ladies, also overflowing.

Unfortunately, men's underwear in America is seldom this picturesque.

Men's briefs, in general, are functional and triple stitched for wear. Seen on the line, in conjunction with ladies' corsets, reinforced by Bethlehem Steel, a sobering prospect looms. American Gothic.

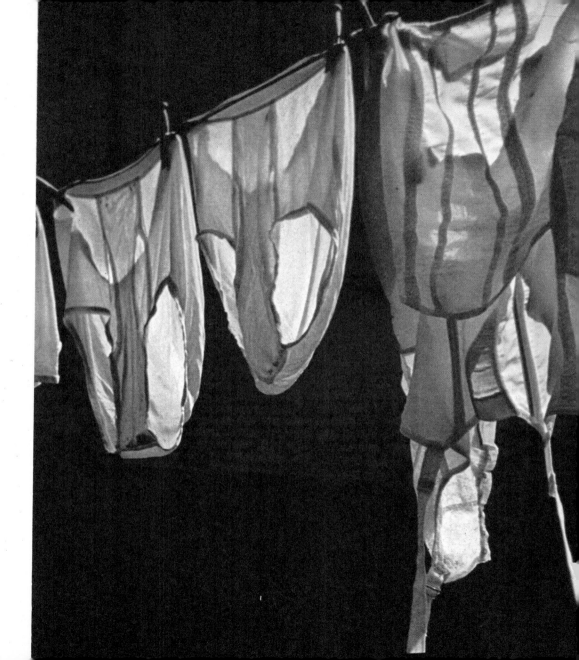

It was in the West that I saw the prescribed underwear of a religious group. These garments, on the line, fall into Old Testament drapes like something from a child's story of the Bible. They are knitted combinations, with round necks, modest sleeves, and legs halfway down to the knees. The men have fly fronts, the ladies have drop seats, some have initials embroidered in the crotch.

Carter's little saints are everywhere; you just have to look for them.

A time

to be christened,

There are lines to span a lifetime,

A time to play,

A time to have a family,

A time to die.

Monday is wash day, right across the country.

In the beautiful Heber valley of Utah, there was a woman who washed her clothes and hung them out every Monday of her life. There came a year when Christmas fell on Monday. All seven of her grown–up children came back home, just to see what she would do. She got self-conscious and just sat. For some reason she took sick. The following Monday was New Year's, but this time she didn't take any chances. She washed her clothes, and hung them out, and never had another sick day in her life.

There was a slightly soiled artist in San Francisco, who dried his clothes on his back, who told me to look for white on white on the clotheslines.

I found a patch on hand–woven linen, more beautiful than anything in the Museum of Modern Art.

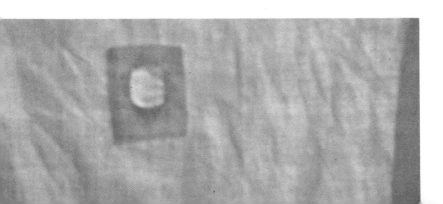

He said to look for sun through sheets.

He told me to find the artists, all working in the same materials—sun, air, and big rectangles of white sheeting—who exhibited in different ways, all clean, functional design.

He told me to watch for the sculpture on the lines, the diapers repeating over and over, like a Greek frieze, perfect parabolas.

"They're disorderly," said the real estate man, stomping out his cigarette in his coffee cup.

There are very strict rules in clothesmanship. True, it's just a job that has to be done, but it must be done well.

It's a hanging crime to take clothes just as they come from the basket.

No matter where the lines go, the rules follow: Hang
socks together, shirts together. Each class hangs together.
There is a lady named Mrs. Bongo, in Minneapolis, who
takes it a step further, she graduates them according to
color.

First get those clothes clean,

then have your line taut.

For mathematical precision and order, consider a rotary drier hung each morning for the last five years with seventy-two diapers, four to a line, so precisely arranged that even the clothespins line up like soldiers.

I found one of the most spectacular examples of order hung on a back street in Boise, Idaho.

I knocked on the front door. A small woman opened it. "Your clothes," I asked, "do you always hang them that way?"

Mrs. Ware was a small woman, but she drew herself up tall. "That's the way my mamma done it, and that's the way I do it."

Mrs. Ware was a Mormon; these people really care. Beginning with the smallest garment, baby's socks, they progress on to the next in length, regardless of time or effort to make the finished line a perfect right-angled triangle.

"My family was very starchy," Mrs. Ware told me. "On the way home from church we always took a walk around town to look at other people's clotheslines. That was how we chose our friends."

This proves that there is status in clotheslines.

If you are making a conventional tour of the nation, following the arrows on the scenic drives, staying behind ropes in historic houses, hustling to catch up with the tour guide, you will not need my

Regional Clothesline Guide to America.

Kansas

Maine

When you go through a paling fence, then a hemlock hedge, screening a small airless area to find a small clothesline hiding in the company of cat's dishes, garbage cans, and deposit bottles, terrified of property values, where are you?

New Canaan, Connecticut.

In Vermont you pass farmhouse after farmhouse with the wash hanging under the porch.

On a brilliant July day I asked a Vermont woman, "Why don't you hang your wash out in the yard?"

"Well," she explained patiently as if any fool should know, "summer's so short it hardly matters."

There are sheets lying on the wind in the Dakotas, and another whole line of shadows underneath.

Oklahoma

"Sure they're clean," said the dramatist. "And they've got suspense, but there's no drama in them."

Call it anthropomorphism to read human traits into inanimate objects, but I saw a lot of human emotions on the lines.

Nightshirt pendent

Nightgown couchant

Patience

Impatience

Loneliness

Companionship

Flamboyance

Austerity

Elation

Depression

Insecure

Confident

Hope

Despair

Virtue in Massachusetts

Vice right across the nation:
   the stolen towel

Pessimism in Pittsburgh

Optimism in Darien

Dottie Calderwood told me, while we
were running for the Vinalhaven ferry
at the end of the trip, why women
leave a line of clothes out overnight.

"If you have a soil,
   A spot, or a stain,
   Leave it to the night,
   The moon, and the rain."

An Alphabet Press Book

Planned, designed, and produced by Helen Mather and Stefan Salter.

The type is Baskerville.
The paper is Finch Textbook Offset.

The Alphabet Press wishes to thank Bill Thompson of Doubleday, Ralph Heilman of the Canfield Paper Co., Pete Markovitch of Capper Engraving, and Al Oliver of American Book–Stratford Press, for their help in producing this book.